Thankfulness: The Secret Ingredient

D. Mckinnon

This book or parts thereof may not be reproduced in any form, stored in a retrieval system, or transmitted in any form by any means – electronic, mechanical, photocopy, recording, or otherwise – without prior written permission of the publisher, except as provided by United States of America copyright law.

Unless otherwise noted, all Scripture quotations are from the Holy Bible, Modern English Version. Copyright © 2014 by Military Bible Association. Used by permission;

King James Version of the Bible;

New International Version (NIV). Copyright © 1973, 1978, 1984, 2011 by Biblica, Inc. Used by permission of Zondervan. All rights reserved worldwide. www.zondervan.com. The "NIV" and "New International Version" are trademarks registered in the United States Patent and Trademark Office by Biblica, Inc.

Copyright © 2018 Danelle Mckinnon

All rights reserved.

ISBN-13: 978-0578404547
ISBN-10: 0578404540

DEDICATION

This book is dedicated to Christ Jesus, I exist to serve and glorify Him. Because of His saving grace, I am who I am. I pray this book touches the life of each person that reads it and helps bring them closer to God.

CONTENTS

	Acknowledgments	i
1	Introduction	1
2	Begin the Day Thankful in Prayer	3
3	Get Excited to Give Thanks	6
4	The Attitude of Thankfulness	9
5	Focused Gratitude	13
6	Live Beyond Feelings and Emotions	16
7	Fight with Positive Purpose	20
8	Make Time for Peace and Rest	26
9	Comparison's Lies	30
10	Thankfulness in the Ordinary	35
11	Detours and Delays	40
12	Sacrifice of Thankfulness	45
13	It's A Command	49
14	Anxiety and Worry, No More!	55
15	Check Your Heart Health	61
16	Plant and Grow	66

ACKNOWLEDGMENTS

Thank you to Jesus, for loving me beyond me.

Thank you to my family for all your support and prayers.

Bethany, thank you for speaking and writing into me.

A special thank you to each person reading this book. May you be blessed and grow more thankful daily.

1
INTRODUCTION

Could thankfulness and gratitude be the missing ingredient to creating a peaceful and charming life? If you study your life closely enough, you will find that the pursuit of material gains and even millions of dollars, don't provide true happiness. There are rich people who are owners of multi-million-dollar businesses, whose lifestyles are seemingly everything anyone could ever want, yet they take anti-depressants just to escape feelings of depression. On the other hand, there are other people living in extreme poverty, who sleep well, enjoy life, and have a joyful and happy countenance.

What is the difference between the two? Thankfulness.

Typically, daily we can find people who are negative, complaining, and generally unhappy. It would seem they lack something that is vitally important as they never seem satisfied. Ever been around a person who focuses on finding the worst-case scenario in every situation? They complain about everything; will complain about anything, and; YES, even will complain about nothing.

They have the tendency to fill even the happiest situations with negativity that steals all the joy from the event. They have not grabbed a hold onto what can change their entire perspective, and that is thankfulness and gratitude.

There are several ways to change a negative focus into a thankful and positive one: Beginning each day thankful in prayer, being excited to give thanks, focusing on thankfulness regardless of situations, changing habits of complaining, checking your heart health and quitting needless comparisons; to name just a few. We don't realize just how much energy we expend to focus on negativity rather than living in a consistent state of thankfulness.

Take a moment and think of how physically and mentally draining negativity is. Think of how it leaves you feeling.

We can live beyond our feelings, emotions and situations to fully live a life of gratitude, on PURPOSE! The thoughts we give time and energy to eventually affect our state of heart and inner being. This is where life's secret ingredient: Thankfulness, becomes the catalyst for change.

We must make the concerted effort to retrain our "natural response to complain" into a nature that thankfully faces each day. This change brings about an attitude of gratitude. We will face each day knowing that we have let go of negativity and begin to walk in the peace and freedom of Thankfulness.

So, let's make the decision and begin that journey, now.

2
BEGIN THE DAY THANKFUL IN PRAYER

No matter what is going on in our lives, no matter what we are praying for, THANKSGIVING can always be added. Beginning each day in prayer and being thankful is a great habit to form.

I encourage you to examine your life, to pay attention to your thoughts and spoken words, to FRAME your day with gratitude, and to see HOW much thanksgiving you express each day.

Make a concerted effort not to murmur and complain. FIND something to be thankful for; no matter how small or large it may be. Work on building your "Thankfulness" muscle! Regardless of how you FEEL about things.

1 Chronicles 23: 30 reads, "They are to stand every morning to THANK and PRAISE the LORD, and likewise in the evening." One way to change our thinking is to purposefully change our perspective about life, issues, situations, problems, etc. Instead of looking for what is "wrong", begin to seek what is right or going well.

It takes much more energy to search for negativity and to keep a negative outlook than being positive. Not to mention, negative feelings and emotions tend to grow rather quickly and permeate every area of life, if you allow them. You will think, speak, and expect negativity if you focus on it. Positivity takes some work but creates an atmosphere of thankfulness that will catch on like wildfire.

Challenge: TODAY, find three things to be thankful for and write them down:

1. One Feature About Yourself You Are Thankful For?
2. One Thing About God You Are Thankful For?
3. One Person You Are Thankful For?

_____

_____

_____

Refer to the reasons you are thankful each time a negative thought comes to mind. Make sure to frame your references for situations and life each day with a thought of thanksgiving. Create the basis for change in your thought process and follow up with the actions.

The more you concentrate and focus on being thankful the easier it will become. Purposefully be determined to move with thanksgiving in ALL things.

It has been said that it takes approximately 21 days to change old habits and create new ones. Let's take the journey of changing what we view as important through the lenses of thankfulness and gratitude. You will not regret it.

Prayer:

Thank You Father, for the way you guide me in prayer. Help me to come to YOU in a spirit of thankfulness before I do anything else. Let gratitude be the foundation of my prayer life. I make the DECISION today to put aside complaining and be thankful instead.

Notes:

_____

_____

_____

_____

_____

_____

_____

_____

_____

_____

_____

_____

_____

3
GET EXCITED TO GIVE THANKS

How often do we thank God? On a day-to-day basis? For the little things? For things we don't realize we have until they are gone? For the things or people, we take advantage of or benefit from? Are we thankful for just having a normal day?

OR, do we only seek blessings or answers from God? Do we only seek God to fix our problems? Do we only ask for what we don't have?

What is our focus?
How do we frame our prayers?
What focus do we view our life with?

If we are honest, we could all work on being more thankful. We should walk through our perceived mundane life with GRATITUDE. When we change the frame of our life to THANKFULNESS, we are a shining light to those around us - even when we do not recognize it.

Thankfulness: The Secret Ingredient

Acts 13:47 reads, "For so the Lord has commanded us, 'I have placed you as a light for the gentiles, that you may bring salvation to the end of the earth.'"

This "light" can be characterized as a kind word, a smile, our response in certain situations, the grace of thankfulness towards a difficult person or situation, a kind deed or gesture, or even a sincere thank you to someone who least expects it.

Thankfulness reframes our thoughts and deeds and allows us to show the love of God to the people we encounter. We stop focusing only on ourselves.

Excitement is vibrant and attractive. Have you ever seen someone smile when they address you or someone near you? Their smile is contagious. Their joy and happiness extend outward to others. A positive and joyful attitude changes the atmosphere of an entire room.

Our thankful demeanor will:

- attract someone to Christ
- help someone to view their day differently
- awaken inner love for one struggling with self-worth
- relieve tension in a difficult situation
- shift a negative focus to one of positivity
- reassure someone struggling emotionally

Think about how you were as a child receiving a gift and what joy it brought to your life. Think of how you thanked the person who gave you the gift. The smile and satisfaction it brought to them. This is the way God feels when we are thankful and frame our day with gratitude.

Challenge: Tell someone you are thankful for them today. Pick someone who will not expect it.

Watch them smile. Remember that feeling!

Prayer:

Father, I am excited to give you thanks. I want to see your works in all situations. Let the light of gratitude shine brightly in me to help others see you. Today, I make the DECISION to be thankful in all things.

Notes:

_____
_____
_____
_____
_____
_____
_____
_____
_____
_____

4
THE ATTITUDE OF THANKFULNESS

Our daily focus and thought patterns point to what our "normal" habits are. We have the tendency to focus on the negative or what we are missing. After a while, these repeated routines become normal behaviors often occurring sub-consciously. Hence, we end up with a continual habit of complaining, murmuring, nitpicking, and negativity.

Ever been around a person who focuses on finding the worst-case scenario in every situation? They complain about everything, anything and yes, even nothing. With a negative focus, even great moments become filled with only concern for why things are not better or with focusing on what is missing. The moment is lost.

Think about how it makes you feel to be in their presence. Think about how it would change your outlook if you were consistently around them daily.

Would it change your perspective? Would it make you feel depressed or ungrateful? Would it make you not want to be around them again?

Would it change your focus to finding the negative?
Would it be difficult to maintain a positive outlook?

Negativity and complaining are counter-productive to living a life of thankfulness. 2 Corinthians 10:5 teaches us to "destroy arguments and every lofty opinion raised against the knowledge of God, and to take every thought captive to obey Christ."

Bottom line – WE have the ability to change negative thought patterns. The power is ours to decide what we allow ourselves to meditate on. Philippians 4:8 reminds us, "whatever is true, whatever is noble, whatever is right, whatever is pure, whatever is lovely, whatever is admirable – if anything is excellent or praiseworthy – think about such things."

We may not be able to control each thought that comes to our mind - BUT - we do control how long the thought stays there. We must be very careful of the thoughts we allow to take root in our minds or grow within our lives – after all we ARE what we THINK.

There are some steps to developing grateful habits:

1. Preparation – Make the conscience effort to look for areas to change negative thoughts, actions, reactions and responses. Think about how you will be grateful and plan how you want to focus on thankfulness.

2. Action – Be determined to correct old negative habits and replace them with thankfulness and positivity. Practice gratitude in your day-to-day life. Make the changes you have decided on – TAKE ACTION.

3. Maintenance – With any habit change, it is easy to become discouraged when you fall short. But, do not stay

there in defeat. Get back on track, start again and maintain your focus.

Challenge: Write down three areas you can commit to being more thankful in:

1. _____

2. _____

3. _____

Take the time to make a concerted effort to continue to be thankful in these areas. Understand that you have the power to exact the change in your life that you seek. Change takes time and you will be successful because you have dedicated your life to become one of thankfulness, positivity and gratitude.

Prayer:

Lord, guide me to a mindset of thankfulness and gratitude. Help me to be mindful in the areas I have decided to change. Give me strength where I am weak. Change is not easy, but I know you will empower me to be successful.

Notes:

5
FOCUSED GRATITUDE

Examine your life. I encourage you to pay attention to what you watch, listen, read, and what you choose to actively participate in. We live in a time when technology and television have become the most popular way for people to enhance their connections, interactions and receive information.

We see time and time again that social media and television broadcasts are overly critical, have a negative focus and depict hurtful interactions. Spending too much time watching negativity or reading negativity can damper our ability to remain positive and thankful.

Ask yourself, how do you feel after reading or viewing these things?

Do you begin to murmur? Do you start to empathize with it? Do you respond with complaints? Have your emotions changed? Does your focus shift?

According to Webster dictionary, the definition of focus is a central point, an attraction, attention or activity.

In other words, our focus is the central belly button of what we pay attention to or base our actions around.

In order to change our focus to thankfulness, we must develop and nurture gratitude in every situation. We must become radical in our thinking. It takes time and intimacy with God to see how blessed we are. As we grow closer to Him, we can drown out negativity and focus on our spiritual intake.

Colossians 3:16 teaches, "Let the word of Christ dwell in you richly, teaching and admonishing one another in all wisdom, singing psalms and hymns and spiritual songs, with thankfulness in your hearts to God." The more we focus on learning God's Word and His promises to us, the more we can frame each day in positivity and gratitude.

Challenge: Consider how much more positive energy and gratefulness you will feel daily, if before you speak, act, respond, make the decision, or react that YOU have already decided to be thankful for the day.

Focus daily on being grateful before any interaction. Decide to be thankful in every situation on PURPOSE.

Seek something to be thankful for each day!

Replace negative thoughts with positive thoughts daily. Spend less time watching negativity on television; don't read negative posts on social media; and don't engage in negative conversations.

Change your negative intake in order to affect your thankful output.

Prayer:

Father, I choose to live thankfully. I boldly declare that my frame of reference each day will be one of thankfulness and gratitude. Thank you for being faithful to give me the power to achieve this.

Notes:

6
LIVE BEYOND FEELINGS AND EMOTIONS

On any given day, we go through many different emotions and feelings. We feel excited, happy, depressed, hurt, angry, sad, discouraged, and a myriad of other intense feelings. But we must learn to manage our feelings rather than allowing our feelings to control us and our reactions.

Even in situations that are out of our control, there are still plenty of reasons to be sincerely thankful. If we decide to wait until we figure out how we "feel" in order to be thankful, we are allowing our emotions to control us. If you take the moment daily to count each blessing and give energy to the positive in your life rather than focusing on problems, your eyes will be opened to the abundance of God's blessings all around you.

Consider how much energy it takes to look for the negative versus living in a state of continual gratitude. Think of how truly draining negativity can be.

When you are willing to live beyond your feelings, God is faithful to give you the necessary strength to continue to do so.

His strength and renewal will lead and guide us to face whatever has shown up in our lives, as Psalms 138:3 reminds us, "In the day when I cried out, You answered me, and made me bold with strength in my soul".

God wants us to think of and focus on positive things. The battle begins within our mind. We control the thoughts we hold on to and act upon. Actively meditate on being thankful! Proverbs 4:23 reminds us to, "Watch over your heart with all diligence, for from it flow the springs of life."

The thoughts we give energy and time to will eventually affect our state of heart and inner being. This is where daily application of gratitude transforms our focus, actions and reactions.

Harboring negative emotions not only affect us mentally, physically and emotionally, BUT it will spill over into our relationships and friendships. Having emotions isn't right or wrong, after all we are human, right? We can't escape that fact. We all experience situations, whether good or bad, that affect our emotions. However, what we chose to do with our emotions can hurt us, others and put distance between us and God.

Negativity will cause us to become cold, distant, and distracted from what is most important. God has given us the power of free will. You and I have the power to control our emotions. We do not have to dwell in a place of negativity or hurt.

Acknowledge the hurt and decide to move forward from it. Remining in hurt or disappointment causes bitterness and defeats our ability to heal. Change is difficult but it is ultimately worth it. Imagine how freeing it will be to let go of negativity and replace those feelings with gratitude.

Challenge: Write down a few negative emotions, you are willing to work towards changing.

_____

_____

_____

_____

_____

Believe that you have made the change in the areas you wrote down and keep striving each day to create a habit of gratitude and thankfulness. Even if you slip up, refocus on the change you have committed to.

Old habits die hard, but a new focus can overpower them.

Make the committed effort to retrain your "natural, first response". We can find freedom in thankfully facing each day, knowing that we can let go of negativity and pressing forward in allowing each day to be a day of thanksgiving.

Being thankful and full of gratitude is a choice.

Prayer:

Lord, I thank you that my emotions and feelings no longer have control over me. I take back control of my reactions and responses. I am thankful and I am going to live each day from thankfulness. I will not wait to see how I feel before I decide how to react. With your help, I will live beyond my feelings.

Notes:

_____

_____

_____

_____

_____

_____

_____

_____

_____

_____

_____

_____

7
FIGHT WITH POSITIVE PURPOSE

There are many voices that we hear daily. However, the most dangerous voice to living thankfully is our very own "inner critic". Often, this condemning voice threatens our focus. We happen to believe more of the negativity we tell ourselves than what others say to us or about us.

The things we tell ourselves can often be deafening and ultimately defeating…

…I failed again
…I am so messed up
…I can't succeed
…I have nothing to be thankful for
…I am not enough
…No one understands me
…I can't do any better
…I have nothing to offer
…I am not important
…No one loves me, and the list of negative speech can go on and on.

Just think – what would you do if someone else spoke these words to you? Would you defend yourself? Would you tell them they were wrong and disrespectful? Would you become enraged or upset? More than likely, we would have choice words for them in our own defense.

Statements such as these tear down our self-esteem, defeat our dreams, kill our inner peace and affect each area in our lives.

So, why it is that we have become comfortable with speaking to ourselves in this manner?

To be honest, we all have private conversations within ourselves daily. How we approach our inner voice and thoughts is critical and it is where we experience victory or defeat. Negativity is a major roadblock or obstacle to changing our focus to facing each day with thankfulness.

Negative words very quickly become self-fulfilling prophecy squeezing out positive focus.

Fight for yourself with a positive purpose.

Silencing our inner critic is one of the hardest challenges we face to changing our perspective. It takes a step of faith to believe that God loves us and has created many talents and strengths within us. We are valuable to God and have the power to speak against our inner critic and feelings of insecurity.

We can decide to fight the good fight of faith. We must preload our thoughts with the Word of God and what He says about us. It is important to understand who we are in relation to God's word. God made us in His image and has made us joint heirs with His son, Jesus Christ.

Isaiah 43:10 reads, "…Do not be afraid, for I have ransomed you. I have called you by name; you are mine.", and Jeremiah 29:11 teaches, "For I know the plans I have for you," "They are plans for good and not for disaster, to give you a future and a hope." God has redeemed us from our past, called us by name, loves us as His own.

His plan for our life gives us a future and hope. We only must believe. God's love for us does much more than any negative thought can. The bible reminds us…

…I am His masterpiece, fearfully and wonderfully made. (Psalm 139:14)

…I am the product of His workmanship in my life. (Ephesians 2:10)

…I am established by His love and power. (Ephesians 3:17-18)

…I am sealed with His promise and love. (2 Corinthians 1:22)

…I am redeemed by the love He freely gives and His grace. (Romans 3:24)

Don't spend energy fighting a battle that is already won.

Often, we spend time trying to achieve what has already been done for us through Christ Jesus. It is hard to believe and accept what He has done for us because we don't feel as if we deserve it.

We struggle with believing His unconditional love for us.

Thankfulness: The Secret Ingredient

Somehow, we think we must be Christians for a long period of time, live a perfect life or must have done a lot of good deeds to gain His love.

Not true, we are loved by Him, based on His decision to love us. Period! Case closed.

Once we grasp this truth and believe it, we can live from a place of thankfulness. Then we can develop an awareness of our thought patterns and recognize that negative thinking doesn't mean what we "think" is true nor do we have to accept it.

Our inner thoughts are likely exaggerated and biased based on our feelings and past experiences. Every time you find yourself responding negatively or speaking negatively about yourself, stop and think with a more positive and accurate statement.

Fighting the negative inner chatter with positive fuel ignites the fire of thankfulness within our lives.

An inner dialogue of thankfulness and gratitude is one of the most powerful postures we can have in response to the love God has shown us.

Challenge: Write (5) positive thoughts about yourself. Do not focus on the past. Leave past mistakes, guilt or shame out of your mind when coming up with this list.

1.

_____

2.

_____

3.

_____

4.

_____

5.

_____

Use this list of positive attributes of yourself as a starting point for each day from here forward. Change your very own perception of yourself.

Realize that you are:

...doing better than you think you are doing.
...learning day by day to be better than you were before.
...growing in knowledge and making better decisions each day.

Prayer:

Lord, we are thankful that you love us and have wonderful plans for our lives. Open our eyes to see the work of your hands in all things. Steady our hearts, quiet our negative thoughts. Help my focus to remain on being thankful and not the negative things going on around me.

Notes:

8
MAKE TIME FOR PEACE AND REST

Have you gotten so busy that all your time seems occupied? Is your schedule overcome with constant running from here to there? Do your days seem to run together, with weeks or months passing before you realize you need a break?

We fly through life at warp speed forgetting to embrace inner peace and rest. Think about it. We get caught up in the hustle of life, focused on our problems and trapped in our on-the-go schedules that never seem to stop.

We can have a "to-do" list of many things to accomplish, a plan for weeks to come and experience unexpected events that completely derail our perspective off track.

A "super-busy" focus chronically drains our life of peace and rest. The focus of spending more and more time on making money, being an overachiever, addictive behaviors (such as "screen time" with cell phones, tablets, social media, television shows and messenger apps), and the pursuit of material things crowd out the time for peace and rest.

Unfortunately, this lack of peace and rest causes chronic stress. Stress tends to strain our lives, stripping away our peace. It ties directly to worry, anxiety, trouble, difficulty, tension and strain. It not only affects us physically and emotionally but also spiritually.

Time is a commodity we all seem to fall short of when we do not have our priorities in the correct order. The lack of time management destroys peace and robs our mind of the ability to be thankful. Setting priorities in life are paramount to what we focus on.

We must acknowledge that being busy does not mean that we are doing well or that we are serving others well. Most especially God or those who are closest to us. The best way to be productive in life is not by cramming so much in that we shut out God. We need to allow rest to take place as God has designed it.

We must recharge. We do not run-on energizer batteries.

It is crucial that we incorporate restful breaks into our self- inflicted busyness in order to be restored and refocus.

No, of course we can't just cancel life!

BUT we can embrace resting in Christ spiritually and physically. In fact, we can rest assured that He will provide us with the rest and restoration we need, if we allow Him.

Psalm 62:1-2 reads, "My soul finds rest in God alone; my salvation comes from him. He alone is my rock and my salvation; he is my fortress; I will never be shaken."
Rest is important to our physical, emotional and spiritual well-being.

Rest will elude us if we consistently strive, toil and remain busy without taking the time for rest and meditation. Our peace is directly tied to the time we spend with God. He wants to replenish our spiritual reserves and our physical reserves as well.

We must focus on not becoming so busy that we cannot find time to support our relationship with God.

Challenge:

1. Believe your value is in WHO you are, not WHAT you do.

2. Do something daily to encourage peace and thankfulness.

3. Don't sacrifice your peace or sanity. Give it to God.

4. Listen to your body. Rest.

5. Allow yourself to enjoy PEACE. Some things can wait.

Prayer:

Father help me to be still and know that you are God. Teach me to trust in you that I am always able to know your peace in my life. Help me to overcome stress and busyness so that I will have more time to be with you. I pray I will have time to reflect on all the ways you have taken care of me and have blessed me.

Notes:

9
COMPARISION'S LIES

Do you find that you compare yourself or your life to others? Your salary? Your home? Your spouse or significant other? Your kids? Your car? Your appearance or your weight?

Are you envious of what others have? Envious of what you perceive is happening in their lives? Do you secretly strive to achieve what others have done? Do you get jealous of what you see in someone else?

To be honest, we cannot be content comparing ourselves to other's lives. Envy and jealousy destroy thankfulness and gratitude. While, we can't completely change the feelings that cause envy, jealousy or comparison, we CAN change the ways we look at our lives to help eliminate dwelling on them.

If not careful, we will find ourselves caught in the trap of constantly comparing ourselves to others. At times the comparisons are not even intentional, they happen out of habit. We spend time sizing our life up to someone else's measures or standards.

Thankfulness: The Secret Ingredient

Listening to what OTHER people deem is better than what we currently have or are experiencing steals our ability to be thankful. We then lose sight of the blessings we DO have.

Comparison is not only physically draining but also spiritually draining. It's an ugly trap robbing us of security, peace and hope.

We must learn to turn a deaf ear to our inner desire to be perfect, better than others and the inner desire to acquire what everyone else would be jealous of.

Galatians 6:4 teaches, "Pay careful attention to your own work, for then you will get the satisfaction of a job well done, and you won't need to compare yourself to anyone else." Paying attention to what pleases God saves us from the stress of meeting someone else's requirements or comparisons for our life.

There are several ways to stop comparing ourselves to others:

1. Put merit in God's Word rather than anyone else.

Seek to intently read, listen to and believe God's Word before you listen to your own opinion, or other's opinions. Our insecurities cause us to compare ourselves to others, to feel more superior. However, God's word says that we are fearfully and wonderfully made. We are His children in Christ Jesus. We have God's measuring stick to live by, and not our own or others. Believe what God says about you and rely on His love to sustain you. You are worthy, you are chosen, and you are set apart. Spend time with God and He will satisfy your deepest desires.

2. Take a personal time out.

Social media, television, magazines, and newscasts feed the need to compare ourselves to others. What we visualize becomes very enticing or damaging. We have the propensity to become enthralled with likes on pictures, seeking after more social media followers and getting caught up in comments or posts. While, social media can be a great way to keep up with friends and family, it can quickly become addictive and detrimental especially if we struggle with comparison issues. Limit social media. Don't check it every day. Realize God has already proved how valuable you are by creating you to be unique and special. He made you specifically for His purpose.

3. Concentrate and act on your strengths.

One of the most effective ways to destroy the need for comparison is concentrating on your strengths and abilities. Think about your strengths. What has God gifted you with? What unique abilities do you possess? Stop focusing on what others are doing. Instead, spend time praying and seeking what God's intent is for you. Seek how to utilize the gifts and strengths He has given to you. Seek after God's will for your life. Allow Him to lead you to the purpose designed uniquely for you. Rejoice and thankfully go forward utilizing what God has given you.

4. Realize that comparison is ALWAYS through tainted lenses.

When comparing ourselves to others, we are focusing on our perceived "worst" and looking at what we believe to be someone else's "best". There are always three sides to every story. What we see. What we think. What the truth is. There are truths under the surface of someone else's "best" that we will never know because we are not privy to their entire life. They could very well be projecting an image of wellness but truthfully be struggling beneath the surface very near a breakdown.

You may have even had someone approach you with compliments or comparisons about what they "see" in your life and inwardly have said these words, "if only you knew…". Realize that situations are not always what they seem on the surface. If you knew the entire picture of someone's life, you may not covet or want what they have or are currently experiencing.

Instead of engaging in comparison, focus on fulfilling the unique role God has for you.

We break free from the jail of comparison by placing our faith and trust in God. He accepts us. Focusing on His grace and love reminds us to be thankful in all things. We are free from using other people as our standard of measure.

Everyone is struggling or suffering from their own problems, whether you are close enough to them to realize it or not. God grants us the grace and strength to move forward with the mindset of thankfulness, even during our own personal struggles. Comparison forces us to focus only on the struggle and our perceived lack.

Our daily perspective is the key to triumphing over comparison. Being thankful and having gratitude helps us to recognize all the blessings and good things we already possess. We must commit our focus to thankfulness each day to leave vain comparisons behind.

Celebrate and be grateful for the advancements you have made in life. Redirect your desires to ones that highlight positivity. Don't dwell in negativity or self-criticism. Take the opportunity each day to find things to be grateful for. Find satisfaction in all that God has blessed you with.

Think of how you can positively influence someone. Change your focus. Think of how blessed you are. No matter how much or little you have, look at your life and be thankful. Each situation you have encountered made you exactly who you are, and God has a purpose for you.

Love who God created you to be.

Prayer:

Father, help me to stop comparing myself to other people. I want to focus on what truly matters, my relationship with you. Help me to be mindful that you created me with purpose and that you love me. I will not waste time seeking what others have. I want to glorify you with my life always. You are my one and only source. I thank you for freedom from comparison.

Notes:

_____
_____
_____
_____
_____
_____
_____
_____
_____
_____
_____
_____
_____
_____
_____

10
THANKFULNESS IN THE ORDINARY

Some of the great things we possess we take for granted. So many things have become convenient for us that we don't realize we have forgotten their importance. Take for instance, all the blessings God has given us that seem insignificant daily due to becoming common place, such as:

Electricity, running water, refrigerators that preserve foods, ATMs, television, cell phones, indoor plumbing, computers, etc. All the modern conveniences that were at one time very hard to come by. We take them as ordinary everyday things or commonplace, instead of being thankful for God's provision.

Webster's definition of ordinary is, "something with no special or distinctive features; normal" or "what is commonplace or standard". The word ordinary is synonymous with usual, standard, typical, common, every day, regular, routine and day-to-day. In our fast-paced society, it is extremely easy to lose track of the blessings we possess. Abundance has caused us to overlook how great and amazing life truly is.

Society's perspective has changed our thoughts and our approach to a life of thankfulness to a perspective focused on acquiring more and more things. The pursuit of keeping up with technology, getting more material things such as cars, homes, clothing, jewelry, etc., and seeking other's approval have drained thankfulness and gratitude from our lives.

We focus on the continual need to get satisfaction from material gain.

This perspective crowds out what is truly important. The beauty of small, ordinary things. The secret to being thankful is changing your frame of perspective away from what don't have to what you are thankful for.

What small things can you be grateful for? What can you do to stay grateful each day? How can you change your mindset to be satisfied with what you currently have? How much do you really take for granted?

1 Thessalonians 5:18 says "be thankful in all circumstances, for this is God's will for you who belong to Christ Jesus." We certainly take for granted just how important the small things really are. Our focus is mainly on the big things that happen such as promotions, great achievements, or the influence we have had on someone by blessing them with a gift.

However, all the ordinary small things are what make our lives the happiest. A sincere thank you note, a smile, a kind word, our close friend calling us, a cool breeze, beautiful flowers, a child's laughter, etc.

We do not realize that without the small things, our lives would not be worthwhile.

Thankfulness: The Secret Ingredient

God has taken time to give us so many things that bless our lives and make it more enjoyable. We must consciously focus on being thankful in all things.

There are ways to change our perspective from always seeking after gaining more things to a perspective of thankfulness.

1. Practicing daily gratitude – write in a journal each day for those things that you are grateful for. Write down people you are grateful for or small things that helped make your day easier. Consider even writing thank-you notes to the people you are grateful for in your life.

2. Make a genuine effort to change your perspective – look at situations with a positive, thankful view. Filter your responses and reactions to people, events and situations to one of positivity. Make the conscious effort to be thankful for the small things in every situation. Don't allow negativity to cloud your view.

3. Find joy in and be thankful for non-material things – focus on things such as laughter, faith, nature, love, music, take long walks, call a friend, etc. Actively seek things to be thankful for that are already in your everyday life.

4. Ask God to show you how to be thankful and to reveal what areas you may be lacking thankfulness or gratitude in. Be willing to embrace simplicity.

5. Don't be afraid to desire what you already have. Focusing on what you currently possess, instead of seeking after what you feel you lack.

You will find it easy to be more thankful when you take inventory of what blessings you possess and seek enjoyment with what God has given you.

Don't fall into the trap of believing that the "more" you acquire the happier you will be. Nothing wrong with having nice things, BUT don't allow the chase (acquiring things) to become your focus.

Challenge: Thankfulness and Gratitude in action. Find one person to say a sincere thank-you too. Make sure it is someone who will least expect it. Thank them for what they do in your life, how they make your life easier or for just being themselves.

- A waiter or waitress
- The usher at church for seating you
- Your spouse or significant other for loving you
- Your friend just for being there
- A stranger for their smile
- A co-worker for being a part of the team.

It is contagious! Being thankful and putting gratitude into our everyday lives helps keep us focused on the small things that we take for granted.

Plus, it attracts others to become focused on what is important as well.

Prayer:

Lord, help me to change my perspective to being thankful for even the small things. Remind me of how great the little things truly are and help me to look back and be thankful for each of them. I want to value all the blessings you have bestowed on me. No longer will I overlook each thing you have given to me. I seek to live each day with the attitude of gratitude.

Notes:

11
DETOURS AND DELAYS

Even the best plans can end up with detours or delays. Have you ever decided to take a road trip? You get in your car, headed in the direction of your destination, only to experience a detour. No driver enjoys having to take a detour from their planned route, adding time and a delay to the plan.

Without a doubt, this detour brings stress, concern and discomfort; maybe even a little anger.

Similarly, we have our lives planned out with our own personal goals and ambitions, usually from early adulthood. These plans could be our desire to be married by a certain age, our desire to be in a prestigious job, wanting our lifestyle to be perfect, etc. To be perfectly honest, we become discouraged when our plans don't work out exactly as we foresaw them.

Of course, we prefer our life path to follow our original plan. We also expect to take the fastest, easiest route free from any delay to achieving our chosen life destination.

Detours and delays are those sudden changes we just don't expect or welcome. They most likely are situations we did not plan for which block progress.

As a result, feelings of wasted time, lack of control, unsure future, frustration, disappointment, anxiety, impatience, and confusion enter our psyche. Negativity can very quickly thwart any semblance of thankfulness or gratitude from our chosen focus.

Fortunately, delays and detours are a part of our Christian lives for a reason.

Yes, you read that correctly.

God allows delays and detours into our perceived perfect plans. There is always a divine reason for them.

In Proverbs 16:9, we read, "In their hearts humans plan their course, but the Lord establishes their steps.", in Proverbs 19:21, we are reminded, "Many plans are in a man's heart, But the counsel of the Lord will stand." We can only see exactly what is ahead of us. God has the ability to see each of the turns in our lives and what is around the corner in our paths. He loves us enough to change, redirect, protect and prepare us for our purpose with greater responsibility and blessing.

It is through these divinely appointed delays that we discover that God is our faithful and true guide.

Jeremiah 29:11 says, "For I know the plans I have for you, declares the Lord. They are plans for good and not for disaster, to give you a future and a hope." For this reason, it is very important for us to stagger not at obeying God when we are faced with a detour or delay.

We don't want to become paralyzed with fear making the mistake of refusing to obey God's direction because the detour is not what we would have chosen.

Delays and detours help to build our patience, spiritual development and maturity. We must trust in the Lord with all our heart, leaning not to our understanding (Proverbs 3:5) and believe God has our best interest in mind. Romans 8:28 further shows, "that God causes everything to work together for the good of those who love God and are called according to his purpose for them."

For example, we can be headed in the right direction but may not be mature enough to do what is necessary once we get to our "chosen" destination. Maybe we need more time to fully develop.

Take the children of Israel, for example. They were promised the land of Canaan and were to enter the land after been released from Egyptian rule. However, once Moses led them to the land of Canaan, he sent twelve spies in to assess the land; assess the strength of the populations within the land; assess the conditions of the land, and to return with samples of the local produce.

Ten of the twelve spies returned showing little faith in what God had promised them, slandering what God had said. These ten men were able to convince the entire nation of the negative report except for the two men who believed God's promises. As a result, what was a temporary detour in the wilderness became a 40-year delay of the Israelites entering the land God had previously promised to them. This was due to lack of belief.

This delay was used by God to make them into a nation of disciplines who were law-abiding, God-fearing and spiritually strong. The transformation turned out to be for Israel's good and was required due to their previous state of being a nation who was fearful, selfish, greedy, idolatrous, carnal and un-believing.

We often gain a new perspective in hindsight of a delay, when we take the time to "look back" and access our personal growth. Reflection is an integral part of reviewing and assessing the detours and delays God utilizes to shape our lives.

There is much to be thankful for and gained from discovering God's provision to strengthen and grow us.

Although, the time spent in delay or detour is uncomfortable, we must change our perspective to see the value in them. We move so quickly in life that we hardly take time to focus on how we get where we are going. We are determined to get there, as fast as humanly possible, wherever there ends up being.

The detours and delays God places in our lives will eventually make perfect sense and produce a response of gratitude if we allow them to work His perfect will in our lives.

When we are experiencing delay, there are some questions we can ask ourselves:

What is God's divine purpose in the delay?
Is there something I am missing that I should seek God for? Have I trusted God with the plans for my life?
Can I patiently await God in the delay?

God's delay does not mean denial for the path of your life. He has not forgotten nor abandoned you. Simply be thankful for what He is doing and focus on its purpose. Have faith and trust that God is with us in the detours of life and be thankful for the outcome it will produce.

Prayer:

God open my eyes to recognize the purpose for delay or detours in my life. Help me to be patient to allow your perfect will to grow me into who you desire me to become. I will look to you for guidance and answers. I am thankful for growth, maturity and for the greater blessing that will come as a result of slowing down and allowing you to direct my path.

Notes:

_____
_____
_____
_____
_____
_____
_____
_____
_____
_____
_____
_____
_____
_____
_____

12
SACRIFICE OF THANKFULNESS

Have you ever witnessed someone receive a gift they were not thankful for? Ever been around an ungrateful person or child? Has someone given you a gift or said thank you and you could sense they did not truly mean it? Maybe it was out of obligation? Maybe they were forced to say it? Whatever the reason, it's not a very pleasant experience.

When a person is grateful or expresses heartfelt thankfulness for something we have done, it feels genuine and special. To hear thank you, or that you are appreciated can brighten your day especially if it is unexpected.

God wants us to proactively thank Him daily. This requires our mindset to change. We must take an honest look at ourselves, becoming aware of just how thankful we truly are. In order to do this, we must realize God is at work for good both in us and through us. We must purposely seek out having a heart that will obey God's truth with gratitude.

1 Thessalonians 5:18 reads, "Be thankful in all circumstances, for this is God's will for you who belong to Christ Jesus." We use so much of our energy complaining and being discouraged when situations don't go as expected. We then look at our circumstances and our perceived lack with eyes of disdain.

But Psalm 50:14-16 teaches us to, "Make thankfulness your sacrifice to God, and keep the vows you made to the Most High. Then call on me in the day of trouble; I will deliver you, and you will honor me."

God has given us an advocate, Jesus Christ. We are constantly receiving the love of God and grace to face life's situations. This love reveals our purpose, and what our focus should be. God wants to show us what He can do in our situations by leading us into thankfulness through our obedience to His word and His will for us.

This obedience is not forced, it is what we must choose for ourselves. We must vow to be thankful because of what God has promised and because of the truth of what we have witnessed. It is easy to become distracted from living in thankfulness. We can become accustomed to the blessings God provides for us forgetting to be thankful and being lazy in having gratitude.

Our thankfulness is very important to God. He views it as a part of worship. Most obviously because He alone is worthy of our thankfulness and gratitude. Being thankful puts your heart in the place to recognize His sovereignty during the midst of difficulty or blessings.

Having a thankful perspective in difficult situations produces patience, trust and faith in God's plans. You will not always "feel" like being thankful in every situation. We are human, after all. It is easy to be thankful when life goes smoothly. But when difficulties arise, we often choose to keep our thanksgiving to ourselves until the problems subside. Thinking that we should only have gratitude when things get better.

We typically want to see what God is going to do or hear what God is saying or see what He will change before we offer Him our thankfulness. But we must remember, being thankful helps to keep us humble, attuned with God's will and obedient to His word. Remaining thankful shows God that while you may not understand all of what is going on, you trust Him to take you through the season and believe Him for the outcome. This is a sacrifice of self.

When you continue to sow sacrificial seeds of thankfulness during painful or hard times, you will reap the harvest of blessings that God intended to grow within your life.

It is eye opening and a relief when we realize the source of all blessings is God, our Abba Father.

The perspective of thankfulness and the expression of gratitude permeates us in such a way that it spills over to everyone we encounter. It becomes our method of communicating and demonstrating the intensity of our thankfulness and love for God.

Thankfulness attracts others sending out waves of joy and gratitude that continue to expand - bringing glory to God, blessing other people, and changing the perspective of those around us. Gratitude and thankfulness become character traits by which God's blessings can be graciously shared with family, friends and others.

Prayer:

Father, help me to see your provision in all of life's situations, good or bad. I trust that you know what is best for me, and that you have a reason for all things. I am thankful and gratitude will flow freely from my heart. I will present a sacrifice of thanksgiving willingly to you, with a heart of joy and gratitude. I believe I will receive blessings for each sacrificial seed of thanksgiving.

Notes:

13
It's A Command

Of course, it is easy to be thankful for the good things in life. But are we truly thankful no matter what? Do we find something to be thankful for regardless of the situation?

Perhaps you have lost your job or have financial struggles. Maybe you have lost a loved one or a close relationship has ended. You could be struggling with health or a hurtful decision. Circumstances can be extremely difficult at times, but we still have much to be thankful for.

For example, look at the life of the Apostle Paul. He was imprisoned in Rome for teaching about Christ. Separated from the other disciples, his friends, brutally beaten, unjustly accused, chained and shackled; but He still knew the meaning of true thanksgiving, while during great tribulation.

While in prison he wrote, "Sing and make music from your heart to the Lord, always giving thanks to God the Father for everything, in the name of our Lord Jesus Christ" (Ephesians 5:19-20).

For Paul, it was a daily reality that changed his life and created within him a joyful and thankful heart. He was able to show gratitude no matter the circumstance. He did not allow the jail cell, brutal beatings or other's opinions to dictate his reactions to negativity. God was still good and was still the focus of his life.

We can follow Paul's example in expressing our gratitude and thankfulness. Thanksgiving is one of the hallmarks of a believer in Christ. We must focus on allowing the spirit of gratitude to warm our heart and permeate our relationships with God and others.

Don't focus on finding faults. An ungrateful heart leads to bitterness, selfishness, and dissatisfaction.

If you take the time to look at the world around you, it is easy to see how lack of gratitude and thanklessness are very common. People are rude to others, and a selfish "me first" entitlement rules personal interactions.

Common courtesy is no longer common and is even scorned. People have become enthralled with themselves, and some even struggle to find a word of thanks or positivity.

Ingratitude can become an act of rebellion against God, if we are not careful.

Romans 1:21 reads, "Yes, they knew God, but they wouldn't worship him as God or even give Him thanks. And they began to think up foolish ideas of what God was like. As a result, their minds became dark and confused." The ungrateful heart unchecked long enough will grow cold and indifferent to God's love and mercy eventually forgetting that we depend on God for all things.

Thankfulness: The Secret Ingredient

We are commanded to be thankful. There are several verses in the bible teaching and directing us towards thankfulness:

- Give thanks to the Lord, for he is good; His love endures forever (1 Chronicles 16:34)

- Give thanks in all circumstances; for this is God's will for you in Christ Jesus (1 Thessalonians 5:18)

- And whatever you do, whether in word or deed, do it all in the name of the Lord Jesus, giving thanks to God the Father through him. (Colossians 3:17)

- Devote yourselves to prayer, being watchful and thankful. (Colossians 4:2)

- I will bless the Lord at all times; His praise will always be on my lips (Psalm 34:1)

- Enter His gates with thanksgiving and his courts with praise; give thanks to Him and praise His name. (Psalm 100:4)

Thankfulness and gratitude are the secret to being content.

Philippians 4:12 reads, "I have learned the secret of being content in any and every situation, whether well fed or hungry, whether living in plenty or in want".

A spirit of thankfulness makes all the difference.

When we come to Christ, it is the beginning of an entire new life perspective. He is with us and helps us to follow His word.

When we turn to him, we discover that it is God that works in us according to His will and His good purpose (Philippians 2:13).

He gives us the power to become grateful and thankful despite our circumstance.

Let's participate in a challenge to see exactly where our thought patterns reside.

Think About It:

Pick (3) things you would normally grumble about daily and write them below:

1. _____

2. _____

3. _____

Over the next 3-4 minutes, think of one thing that is positive in reference to each of the (3) things you have written above. Now write down (3) positive thankful statements in reference to the above list.

Even if it is just the words, "I am thankful":

1. _____

2. _____

3. _____

Thankfulness: The Secret Ingredient

Now consider – was it hard to write the list of negative things you grumble about or was it harder to write a list of reasons to be thankful for the "hard/negative" things.

It requires a change of focus to be thankful in all things.

It comes easily to find fault or point out negative things. Positivity takes practice and focus to implement in our daily lives. We must train our thought patterns and reactions.

We can decide to still thank God even during trials and trouble. Not one of us is exempt from having troubles. Yet, we know that we can thank God, because He has promised to be with us and to help us.

James 1:2-3 says, "Consider it pure joy, my brothers, whenever you face trials of many kinds, because you know that the testing of your faith develops perseverance." God uses trials and tribulations to strengthen us and to grow us into maturity.

We can show the light of God in darkness by our testimony and reactions to everyday life. There are those who watch silently to see how we react and respond in difficult situations in life. How we react can attract someone to a relationship with God.

Acts 28:15 reads, "at the sight of these men Paul thanked God and was encouraged." God can use our life "trouble" to be a blessing to others who struggle with faith in believe in who God is.

Prayer:

Father, help my focus to change to one of gratitude. I want to face life's tests with joy and thankfulness. You are there to help and guide me and I give you thanks. I will be thankful each day.

Notes:

14
ANXIETY AND WORRY, NO MORE!

Continuing to worry and stress over situations is essentially choosing to meditate on negativity and destroys our inner peace. Trusting God means we give up worry, un-necessary reasoning, anxiety and feelings of helplessness and allow His infinite wisdom to lead and guide us. We can rest assured He knows what is best.

Work, family, illness, stress, bills, and even other's actions can put us in a negative place or focus. Anxiety and worry leave us wanting in so many areas that they essentially destroy our ability to be thankful. Proverbs 12:25 states, "Anxiety in a man's heart weighs him down, but a good word makes him glad." We must focus on thankfulness instead of what we do not have answers for.

Once you make the decision that you don't have to carry the worry, burdens, or stress you will experience God's peace, which exceeds anything we can understand.

Believe as Philippians 4:7 reminds us, "and the peace of God, which transcends all understanding, will guard your hearts and minds as you live in Christ Jesus."

We regain our thankful attitude through God's peace. This is done through spending quality time with God and resting on His promises. Resetting our focus toward serenity and peace through our relationship with God can help us regain our focus on living with thanksgiving in all things.

Philippians 4:6 teaches us, "Don't worry about anything; instead pray about everything". Tell God what you need, allow Him the space to work and THANK HIM for all He has done. Be careful not to place God on your own timeline or schedule. He has all things under control and knows exactly the timing that is perfect for our lives.

Be honest with God about what you are feeling and are experiencing. Seek His wisdom and guidance in decisions you need to make. Know that you do not carry the burden alone, for He cares for us and expects us to cast our burdens on Him (1 Peter 5:7). Let go of the desire to struggle with anxiety, worry, questions, thoughts and understand God loves you enough to take what you willingly give to him in exchange for his promises.

There is no need to wrestle with what our situation is, what it could be or what it could have been.

In Deuteronomy 7:6-8 and Romans 5:5-6 we are reminded, "God's love has been poured into our hearts through the Holy Spirit who has been given to us. For while we were still weak, at the right time Christ dies for the ungodly." While we are not perfect, God still pours love into our hearts, and strengthens us when we are weak.

Thankfulness: The Secret Ingredient

At a young age, we learn to be concerned with the who, what, when, where and how of situations. Society primes us to be in control of all things, and if we "slip up" we are labeled a failure. We become so concerned and overwhelmed with having to have all the answers that we forget to be thankful that God loves us and even likes us too.

Letting go and letting God be Himself leads directly to our freedom from worry and anxiety. Thankfulness and gratitude point us to God who has already given us the victory. He tells us this in Romans 8:37, "Yet, in all these things we are more than conquerors through Him who loves us."

Luke 12:25 asks us the question, "which of you by being anxious can add a single hour to his span of life?" Isaiah 26:3 teaches us to fear not that He is the one who helps us. We must stop allowing our minds to run wild with anxiety and regain focus on thankfulness.

Several scripture verses refocus us from anxiety and worry to God's love for us:

Matthew 6:25-27: "Therefore I tell you, do not be anxious about your life, what you will eat or what you will drink, nor about your body, what you will put on. Is life not more than food, and the body more than clothing? Look at the birds of the air: they neither sow nor reap nor gather into barns, and yet your heavenly Father feeds them. Are you not of more value than they? And which of you by being anxious can add a single hour to his span of life?"

Matthew 6:33-34: "But seek first the kingdom of God and his righteousness, and all these things will be added to you. "Therefore, do not be anxious about tomorrow, for tomorrow will be anxious for itself. Sufficient for the day is its own trouble."

Isaiah 41:10 "Fear not, for I am with you; be not dismayed, for I am your God; I will strengthen you, I will help you, I will uphold you with my righteous right hand."

Joshua 1:9 "Have I not commanded you? Be strong and courageous. Do not be frightened, and do not be dismayed, for the Lord your God is with you wherever you go."

Regardless of what we face, there are some steps we can choose to follow to refocus:

1. Realize the difference between concern and worry. Of course, we are supposed to be concerned with what is going on in our daily lives and in the lives of those we love, but we cannot allow it to consume us. Notice that concern focuses on healthy methods of coping and solving issues. Worry and anxiety is focused on the problem and not seeking a solution.

2. Recognize that worry and anxiety do nothing to help you mentally, physically or spiritually. Your time is wasted, and your focus is deterred by situations that may not even happen and are completely useless. It is not healthy to allow anxiety and worry to consume your time. Your health will suffer, your mental status will become stressed, and your spiritual health will be embattled with fear. Utilize the time for seeking God's solution for the problem.

3. Choose not to dwell on negative thoughts that cause anxiety and worry. Invite God into all your situations knowing that He can and will reveal a better plan and/or solution. Be thankful that He is faithful and is willing to work in each of the situations you face. Trust that God

wants the best for you and will empower you to turn situations over to Him. Believe that you can leave problems in His capable hands.

4. Guard your heart and your mind as Proverbs 4:23 teaches. Be focused on the Word of God, be careful of what you are paying attention to, and be mindful of what you allow to utilize your time. Plan to be thankful and release everything to God when you cannot handle it. Don't be tempted to define your worth by your successes or failures. Spend time in prayer.

Act It Out: Decide on (3) areas and write them down that you surrender to God today.

1.
_____
_____
_____

2.
_____
_____
_____

3.
_____
_____
_____

Prayer: Father, help me to release each situation I worry over. Forgive me for being anxious and not believing your promise to take care of me. I will focus and release to you what I cannot handle. Thank you for caring and loving me.

Notes:
_____
_____
_____
_____
_____
_____
_____
_____
_____
_____
_____
_____
_____
_____
_____
_____
_____
_____
_____
_____
_____
_____

15
CHECK YOUR HEART HEALTH

Ever heard, "You are what you eat?" or "I think therefore I am?" It is the same spiritually with your heart. You are what you harbor in your heart. The "heart" is the most important part of who we are that we possess. Our heart not only houses our experiences, knowledge, skills but also governs what we find to be most important.

If we were to be able to visualize just how much thankfulness resides in our hearts, we may be surprised to find out it is not as much as we think or would like there to be. It is so very easy for us to get bogged down in what we are doing or what is happening to us so that we forget life's special ingredient: thankfulness.

The more we focus whole heartedly on being thankful and having gratitude, the more we become aware of the depth of God's love for us. Thankfulness gives us the capacity to be more thankful, and more grateful. It causes us to learn thankfulness so deeply that it becomes our natural reaction and response.

Psalms 33:21 says, "For our heart shall rejoice in Him, because we have trusted in His holy name." and Colossians 3:15 reads, "Let the peace of Christ rule in your hearts, since as members of one body you were called to peace. And be thankful." God gives us the gift of thankfulness and it dwells within our hearts if we are willing to change our perspective.

Cultivating thankfulness takes exact purpose and focus. It is more than just reciting what we are thankful for around the table at thanksgiving dinner with our family and friends. We must remain focused on its heartfelt spiritual significance. Being thankful in all things is not easy to do, but it is essential to realizing God's will in our lives.

Are you thankful for your present situations?

Are you thankful for how God made you?

Are you thankful for the growth God has caused in you?

Have you allowed complaining and negativity to consume your focus?

We can train our heart to be thankful by accepting God's gift of gratitude and allowing it to grow. We can make the choice to dwell on thankfulness which brings about contentment within our life instead of sowing seeds of complaining and discord.

We are all in need of a blessing, an answer, a breakthrough, or a miracle in some cases. The enemy fights our hearts with discouragement, lies and hurts. His focus is to destroy our joy, inner peace, and our power.

As we focus on our spiritual heart health, we must bring the attention back to our lifestyle of thankfulness, gratitude, worship, praise and reverence for God.

This creates an atmosphere for our heart to be strengthened in the presence of God.

The more we focus on thankfulness the less room our heart will have for jealousy, selfishness, self-centeredness, greed, strife, anger, bitterness, complaining, negativity, comparison etc.

It takes time and effort to develop a thankful heart.

Unfortunately, many people think they are automatically thankful because of how we react when life is going well, or the façade they put on for others around them.

However, as soon as the situation changes, they quickly forget thankfulness exchanging it for negativity and finger-pointing. Blaming becomes the go-to reaction.

Your dreams, desires and passions live in your heart. Just like your physical body, if your heart dies, then your body dies. If your spiritual heart dies, then so does your ability to be truly thankful. Protect and nurture your heart with the knowledge of God, acceptance of His son Jesus, and allow the Holy Spirit to lead and teach you. Become connected to other people who exude thankfulness in their lives.

An unhealthy heart impacts every area of your life. Your family, friends, ministry, career, legacy, dreams, vision, interactions, reactions, etc. A toxic heart affects and threatens our thankfulness. The enemy uses all types of attacks to sicken our hearts – disappointment, discouragement, disillusionment and disbelief.

Think about the last time your heart was attacked.

How did you respond?

Could a thankful outlook have changed your reaction?

Were there areas you could have been more thankful?

What prevented you from being more thankful?

If you do not like your answers, remember all is not lost.

You have the opportunity to focus on positivity and thankfulness and can make a 180 degree turn around in perspective. Focus on being more thankful one step at a time, one day at a time.

Cultivate THANKFULNESS on purpose:

Speak it!

Words are very powerful. They give us the power to encourage, bless or discourage and tear down. Never underestimate the power of thankful speech. We should focus on speaking gratitude on purpose each day. Speak out loud daily at least 3 to 5 things you are thankful for. You will notice your heart and attitude begin to change towards your life, your situations and the people in your life.

Look for it!

Seek things to be thankful for. At first this will be difficult, because it is not what we are accustomed to spending our time doing. However, making this an active daily practice will change your heart's intentions. You will begin to notice what is right and will focus on the good in situations. You will begin to retrain your vision and heart to seek after what makes thankfulness your authentic core of being.

Prayer: Thank you God for helping me to change my perspective to being thankful instead of complaining and worry. I release to you each area of doubt for the assuredness of your love in my life. Open my eyes to see what is important to you and help me to be thankful as you would have me to be.

Notes:

16
PLANT AND GROW

Think about a farmer and how much planning and preparation goes into planting a crop and reaping a harvest. He or she must proactively approach and strategize every phase to ensure their work is not in vain.

They start with the soil preparation, they maximize their harvest potential by selecting and planting the right seeds, they fertilize, water and weed the growing crops, and finally, they work hard to harvest what they have grown. This does not occur over a few days; it takes weeks and/or months to reap the benefit of their labor.

Isaiah 30:23 reads, "He will also send you rain for the seed you sow in the ground, and the food that comes from the land will be rich and plentiful." As we plant or sow into our lives, we must be careful what we use as our "seeds" and be thoughtful enough to allow God to "water" the seeds in our lives.

We must be as meticulous as the farmer in changing our lifestyle to one that always encompasses thankfulness. It takes a daily effort to remain positive and thankful.

Our seeds are the words we speak. Words we verbalize or speak out loud are very important. Ephesians 4:29 (NIV) teaches, "Do not let any unwholesome talk come out of your mouths, but only what is helpful for building others up according to their needs, that it may benefit those who listen."

We must actively speak seeds of thankfulness and affirmation into our lives and other's lives daily. The seeds we plant are those that we shall reap.

Hurtful, contentious seeds will grow into negative output.

Joyful, thankful seeds grow into positive output.

Be intentional! Include positive daily seeds of affirmation in what you speak such as:

- I am grateful for who God created me to be.
- I am empowered, driven, innovative and blessed.
- I will remain positive in all things.
- I am thankful for who God has placed in my life.
- I am thankful for growth and maturity.
- Whatever has happened or happens, I remain thankful.
- I am secure, not shaken, joyful, content and steady.
- I am not defined by my failures or successes.
- I am not condemned or shameful. My past is not who I am.

Change negative conversations around you by interjecting positivity. Decide to love and laugh daily.

Look at yourself the way God sees you.

Believe that you are forgiven and are God's masterpiece.

Challenge: Write (5) affirmations that you will speak today and cultivate into your life!

1.
_____
_____
_____

2.
_____
_____
_____

3.
_____
_____
_____

4.
_____
_____
_____

5.
_____
_____
_____

Prayer: I thank you God, that you are awakening thankfulness within me. Help me to find ways to creatively thank you by using the gifts and talents that you have given me. I will plant seeds of thankfulness and gratitude in my life. I will speak words that build up and not tear down. I start here and today. I am thankful for all that you have given me and for your grace. I decree that I will show your goodness to all that I encounter. I open my heart to you and my ear to your Word. I have found the joy of thankfulness in my life.

Notes:

www.ingramcontent.com/pod-product-compliance
Lightning Source LLC
Chambersburg PA
CBHW070856050426
42453CB00012B/2243